AF582223

Contents

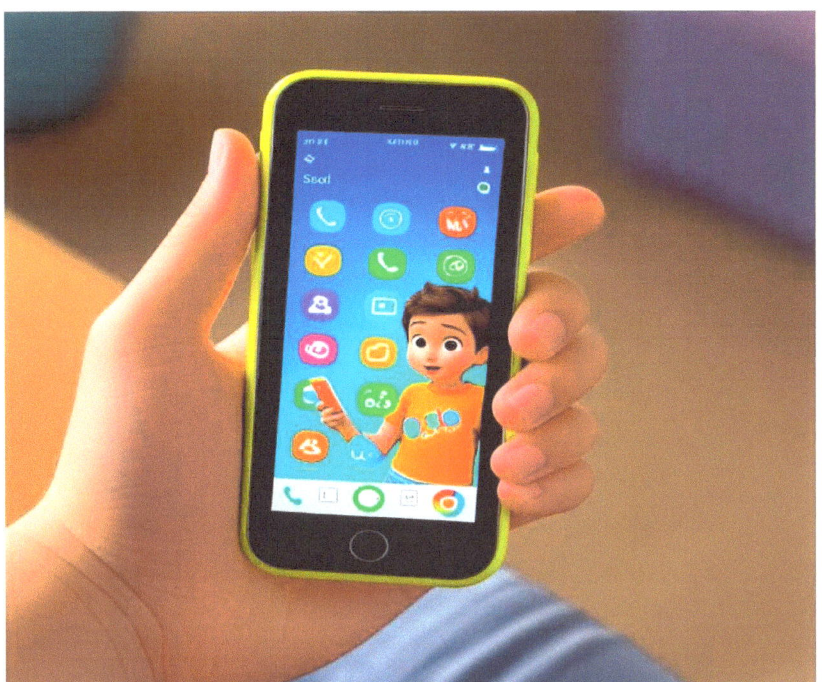

1. Backbiting Will Backfire

Tom and Som were friends so true,
But Tom had a habit, through and through,
He'd talk behind others' backs,
Criticizing, pointing out their cracks.

His parents warned him, "Please refrain,
Backbiting only brings you pain."
But Tom's words, like arrows, flew,
And soon enough, his trait just grew.

One day on the phone, Tom did call,
He and Som talked, had a ball.
But when the chat came to an end,
Tom forgot to hit end, my friend.

He kept on talking, unaware,
Backbiting Som without a care.
He called him weak, he called him wrong,
Said things he'd never say all along.

But Som was listening, heard it all,
The hurtful words that made him fall.

His heart was shattered, trust was gone,
Their friendship ended, just like that, gone.

Moral:
So listen close, take heed, beware,
Backbiting's venom is hard to repair.
Look for the good, and let flaws slide,
Or you might find your friends turn aside.

2. Technology: The grass with a bright side and dull side

Ram and Shyam, both friends so true,
But their lives were different, as you'll see through.
Ram was royal, with wealth untold,
A funky cellphone, a car of gold.

Shyam, on the other hand, was poor,
But clever and witty, with wisdom galore.
One day they planned an excursion bright,
To explore the woods from morning to night.

But alas, they lost their way out there,
Deep in the woods, without a care.
Ram's royal watch stopped with a flick,
The battery died, and the pointer went sick.

Ram panicked, his tech no longer worked,
His swanky gadgets left him irked.
But Shyam, with a smile, used a simple trick:
He took a stick and watched the shadow flick.

Facing the sun, with arms spread wide,
He found the direction, no need to hide.
Ram grew tired, his energy drained,
His royal life had made him vain.

He’d left his car, no engine to hum,
While Shyam walked on, steady and numb.
Shyam, used to walking far and wide,
While Ram's laziness made him slide.

Ram had a lighter, always on hand,
But Shyam made fire with stones on the sand.
Ram’s cellphone went missing too,
But Shyam had a mirror—an old trick, true!

With the sunlight reflected just so,
He helped the helicopter spot the glow.
The smoke from the fire, the mirror’s bright shine,
Guided the rescue team just in time.

Moral:
Technology’s great, no doubt, it's true,
But too much of it can makes us lazy too.
Sometimes the simplest ways are best,
To solve our problems, and pass the test.

3. More Humane than Human

Shane and Jane, two racers fast,
Raced down the road, both keen to last.
But on the path, a man did lie,
Blood flowing, he was near to die.

Shane sped past with barely a glance,
Focused only on his chance.
But Jane saw the man in need,
And with a heart full of good deed,

She stopped her car and took him in,
Rushed to the clinic through thick and thin.
The man recovered, strength regained,
And soon his identity was explained.

The injured one, a minister's son,
Whose life was saved by what she'd done.
Grateful, he rewarded Jane,
For showing kindness without gain.

Meanwhile, Shane, in regret, did stew,
Wishing he'd done what Jane would do.
For in the end, it's clear to see,
That compassion makes us truly free.

Moral here, simple and true:
It matters more what we choose to do.

To be humane, more than just human,
Is a gift we give, to all we're movin'.

4. Non-attachment to results of action – key to happiness

Ricky and Vicky, both friends so true,
Set out for exams that they had to do.
Ricky gave one with great confidence high,
Believing success was within his sight.

He felt so sure that he would succeed,
But before results, he took the lead.
He gave another exam, a school far better,
His hope was high, his heart was set like a letter.

Vicky, full of confidence too,
Was sure he'd pass, his faith never blew.
With a little bit of worry, he chose to play,
He spent time with friends, and passed the day.

When the first results came out, Ricky was thrilled,
He passed the test, his dream fulfilled.
But Vicky, alas, by a whisker missed,
The marks were too low, his hopes dismissed.

Ricky soon learned, to his delight,
The second exam went well, his future bright.
He joined the best school in the land,
Ecstatic, with success in his hand.

But Vicky, dejected, felt the sting,
He focused too much on the result of one thing.

The exam was fine, but the outcome he sought,
Tied him to worry, and happiness was for naught.

Moral:
We must work with effort, without attachment in mind,
But the outcome's not ours, it's not for us to bind.
Do your best, but let the result be,
For non-attachment brings peace and sets the heart free.

5. The Tale of Maya and Kaya

Maya and Kaya, two girls so bright,
One lived in luxury, the other in plight.
Maya was born to riches and fame,
But life wasn't perfect—she couldn't claim the same.

Her mother was sick, in need of her care,
But Maya would turn away, pretending not to be there.
She said, "I'm too busy with my studies today,"
Yet lamented aloud, "I can't focus, come what may!"

Kaya, on the other hand, had so little to call,
Her family was poor, yet she gave her all.
Her father's small shop took much of her day,
But she found time for books and work, come what may.

She never complained, though times were tough,
She took care of her parents, and still had enough.
Her heart was content, her spirit was bright,
She saw each challenge as a chance to take flight.

Maya, despite wealth, could not find peace,
Her dreams were unfulfilled, her stress never ceased.
She couldn't succeed, nor keep her family well,
Her own frustrations made her life a hard shell.

But Kaya, so humble, rose high in her field,
Her career blossomed, her success was revealed.
More importantly, she gave joy to her kin,
Her love for them was the greatest win.

For Kaya knew happiness doesn't come from gold,
It's in seeing the blessings in stories untold.
A smile from her parents, a laugh from her heart,
Made Kaya's life richer than any material art.

Moral:
Look for the good in the trials you face,
For every tough moment is a chance to embrace.
Happiness isn't in what we own or see,
It's in how we respond, and how we choose to be.

6. Unconditional Love

Cris and Ram, both friends so true,
Cris a farmer's son, Ram an orphan too.
Cris was bright, with studies his fame,
Soon he went abroad, to rise in the game.

In a foreign land, with wealth to gain,
He sent money home, to ease his parents' pain.
But work and life kept him away,
Though his love for them never did sway.

Ram, though smart, could not afford
The higher studies that he'd once adored.
He worked at a store, day by day,
But his heart was kind, in every way.

While Cris sent funds from lands afar,
Ram was there, like a guiding star.
He'd visit Cris's parents, bring them care,
Bringing medicine, showing he'd share.

One day, Cris's father asked in trust,
"Could you dig the backyard, as I must?"
Ram agreed, with a willing hand,
To help his friend's family, as best he can.

One fine morning, Ram found them both dead and gone,
His heart sank deep, grief stretched long.

But then, as memories filled his mind,
He recalled the words that had been kind:

“Dig the backyard,” they’d said before,
And so he dug, his heart full of lore.
Beneath the earth, a treasure he found,
A sparkling necklace, riches unbound.

Half he gave to those in need,
An orphanage filled with love and creed.
The rest he kept, a modest sum,
But his heart had learned what love had become.

For Cris, though wealthy, could not replace,
The warmth and care, the loving embrace.
Parents need more than gold or fame—
They need support, love, and someone to claim.

Moral here, simple and clear,
It’s not just money that parents hold dear.
They need your time, your unconditional love, your touch;
For that's the gift that means so much.

7. Not having the best situation but seeing the best in every situation is the key to happiness.

Ram and Shyam, two friends so true,
One rich, the other, not much to view.
Ram had wealth, a life of ease,
But his mother's health was far from peace.

She called for help, but Ram would say,
"I'm busy with studies, I cannot stay."
Yet, as he studied, his mind would roam,
Worrying that his mom felt alone.

Shyam, born poor, had less to find,
But he worked hard and stayed kind.
His parent's love was all he had,
But Shyam was content, never sad.

He studied with care, despite the lack,
And helped his parents, always on track.
No complaints, no cries of despair,
He lived each day with love and care.

Ram, however, kept feeling blue,
His life seemed bleak, though it wasn't true.
He couldn't focus, couldn't see,
That happiness comes from being free.

Shyam rose high, both in life and career,
His parents smiled, their hearts sincere.
With love and patience, he found his way,
A content soul, each and every day.

The moral is clear, it's easy to see:
Happiness comes from being content and free.
Not from wealth or endless gain,
But from love, care, and peace in the brain.

8. The Seed of Wisdom

In a quiet garden, a seed lay so small,
A little boy named Ravi noticed it all.
He bent down and asked, "What should I do?
Should I leave it alone or water it too?"

The wise old tree, with branches so tall,
Spoke softly to Ravi, "Come closer, do not stall.
You see, my young friend, this seed must grow,
But first, it needs care, love, and to know,

That every little seed has a path to follow,
Its purpose is clear, it's not one to swallow.
Just like the seed, you too must do,
The work that is yours, be steady and true."

Ravi thought for a moment, and then understood,
To take care of his task was always good.
He watered the seed, and as it grew tall,
He knew in his heart that duty comes first of all.

Moral:
Just like the seed, we must focus on our duty, without worrying about the end result. Doing what we are meant to do with love and care helps us grow.

9. The Brave Little Bird

In a bright blue sky, a bird took her flight,
Soaring through clouds, with all of her might.
But soon she got tired, and started to fall,
"I'll never fly high again," she thought, feeling small.

Down in the forest, wise old owl sat,
And noticed the bird, feeling just like that.
He hooted and said, "Don't worry, little one,
Let go of the worry, your journey's not done."

"You see, little bird, to fly is your fate,
But you must not be attached to the flight's rate.
It's not about soaring, or how high you rise,
But the joy in the journey, and how you realize—

That all actions you take, don't cling to their end,
Just fly with the wind, let your heart transcend.
Detach from the fear, and from the result,
In freedom, you'll find, there's nothing to halt."

The bird flapped her wings, took off with a cheer,
Now free of the worries that once made her fear.
She soared through the sky, light as could be,
And found that detachment brought her so much glee.

Moral:
Like the bird, we can live with joy and freedom when we do things without being overly attached to the outcome. It's the journey, not the destination, that matters.

10. The Painter's Peace

A painter named Maya, with colors so bright,
Had a canvas before her, ready for light.
But she felt unsure, "What if it's wrong?
What if the colors just don't belong?"

From behind her, a voice spoke out clear,
It was Jane, with a smile ear to ear.
"Maya, my friend, listen to your heart,
Paint with pure love, and let that be your start.

Don't worry about praise, don't fret about fame,
Let your heart guide you, and you'll win the game.
When you do your best with no thought of gain,
You'll find peace within, and joy will remain."

Maya took her brush, with love in her hand,
She painted with care, as best as she can.
She didn't seek praise or worry about the end,
She worked with pure heart, and joy did transcend.

The painting was perfect, full of delight,
But the true masterpiece was her peaceful sight.

Moral:
When we act from a place of love and without concern for reward or recognition, we find true peace and joy in what we do. It's the purity of heart that makes our actions meaningful.

11. The Little Elephant's Patience

In the jungle, young Giri, an elephant so small,
Was trying to reach the highest tree, but couldn't stand tall.
He pushed with his trunk, he tugged with his feet,
But the tree was too tall—oh, what a defeat!

His friend, the wise tortoise, watched from afar,
And said, "Don't worry, Giri, you'll go far.
Patience is key when you face a tough climb,
It may take a while, but you'll be just fine."

"Like the river that flows, slow but so sure,
Or the mountain that stands, steadfast and pure,
Patience will guide you, just take your time,
Success will come, when you learn to climb."

Giri paused and took a deep breath,
He stopped feeling rushed and abandoned his stress.
Slowly but surely, with each little stride,
He reached the top of the tree, so full of pride.

Moral:
Patience is a strength. No matter how big the challenge, when we persist with a calm heart, success comes in its own time.

12. The Brave Little Lion

In the jungle, a lion named Leo was bold,
But when darkness fell, he felt quite cold.
The sounds of the night gave him a fright,
He wondered if he could face the dark night.

One day, he asked Denis, "How can I be strong?
How do I face fears that feel so long?"
Denis smiled kindly and spoke with grace,
"Courage isn't the absence of fear you face.

Courage is knowing, when fear does appear,
You stand tall, you trust, and you persevere.
Fear will come, but you must stand your ground,
The courage within you is where strength is found."

With Denis's words in his heart so true,
Leo faced the night, and the darkness withdrew.
He walked through the jungle, brave and so free,
For courage isn't the absence of fear—it's simply to be.

Moral:
Courage doesn't mean we're never afraid—it means we face our fears with strength and trust in ourselves.

13. The Mountain and the Little Ant

A tiny ant, with legs so small,
Climbed a mighty mountain, standing tall.
She climbed and climbed, but felt so weak,
The peak was far, and her journey bleak.

She stopped and thought, “It’s too much to bear,
This mountain is huge, and I can’t get there!”
But a wise old fox, who passed her way,
Spoke with a smile, “Don’t give up today.”

“Even the tallest mountain, high and grand,
Is climbed by the tiniest step of the hand.
Small actions, repeated, lead to success,
So keep moving forward, don’t second guess.”

The ant took a breath and began to climb,
Step by step, taking her time.
With patience and effort, day after day,
She reached the top—what a glorious display!

Moral:
Small, steady actions lead to great things. Even the longest journey begins with one simple step. Be persistent, and the mountain will seem smaller.

14. The King and the Golden Necklace

A king had a necklace, made of pure gold,
It sparkled and shone, a sight to behold.
He loved it dearly, and never let go,
But one day, a thief came, swift as a shadow.

The king was heartbroken, his joy turned to fear,
For his beloved necklace had disappeared.
He cried to Robert, "What should I do?
I've lost my treasure, what's left to pursue?"

Robert smiled kindly, His eyes full of grace,
"Do not worry, my friend, for material things have no place.
Your joy should not rest on what can be lost,
For true happiness is not tied to what's tossed."

"Detach from the gold, the jewels, and fame,
And find peace within, that's your true aim.
When you seek within, and not in the things outside,
You'll find happiness, no longer to hide."

The king thought for a moment, and then he understood,
That true treasure lies in the heart, not in the wood.
He let go of his worry, and found peace anew,
For detachment is freedom, and happiness too.

Moral:
True happiness comes from within, not from material possessions. Detach from what you can lose, and find peace in your own heart.

15. The Farmer and the Seeds

A farmer named Dev, with hands worn and rough,
Worked hard on his field, but things were tough.
The rain didn't come, the sun was too hot,
His crops were failing, his hope starting to rot.

One day, he asked Mahadev, "What should I do?
I've planted the seeds, but they just won't grow through!"
Mahadev smiled gently and said, "My friend,
Have faith in your effort, and don't let it end."

"Seeds need time, and patience to rise,
You cannot rush the sun or the skies.
Work hard, but trust, and let go of your doubt,
Faith in your actions will bring the result out."

Dev took the advice, and worked with care,
Planting his seeds, day by day, with prayer.
Soon the rains came, and the crops began to bloom,
His faith and effort cleared the gloom.

Moral:
Effort and faith go hand in hand. We must do our part and trust in the process, knowing that patience and hard work will eventually bear fruit.

16. The Wise Deer

A deer in the forest, graceful and light,
Loved to jump and run, day and night.
But one day, he heard of a grand feast,
A banquet of fruits, to say the least.

He ran through the woods, with speed in his stride,
But Crys appeared and stood by his side.
"Why are you rushing, my friend, so fast?
Don't let desire control you, or you'll be outclassed."

"Desires are like rivers, they rush and they race,
But they can drown you, if you don't set the pace.
Discipline is key, to stay calm and true,
Control your desires, let wisdom guide you."

The deer stopped, thinking over Crys's word,
He slowed down, his heart no longer stirred.
He learned to be mindful, with patience in place,
And found that balance brought him true grace.

Moral:
Discipline and control over one's desires bring inner peace. When we act with self-restraint, we find balance in life.

17. The Strong, Silent River

A mighty river flowed through the land,
It rushed over stones, with a roar so grand.
But Richard appeared, beside its flow,
And said, "My friend, please help me, its about you I want to know…"

"The river is strong, it rushes and bends,
But it never stops—its flow never ends.
Yet its true strength lies, not in the noise,
But in its steady movement, in the quiet choice."

"Like the river, you must stay true to your way,
Let your actions speak, and not what you say.
Strength lies in patience, in being unbowed,
Not in loud rushing, but in being proud."

The river slowed its rush, and grew serene,
Flowing calmly through valleys so green.
It found its power in silence and grace,
Moving forward, with peace in its trace.

Moral:
True strength comes from being steadfast, calm, and patient. Like the river, we must move through life with quiet determination and inner peace.

18. The Little Cloud

Up in the sky, a little cloud floated by,
Puffy and white, so free, it could fly!
It boasted and bragged, "Look at me go!
I'm the biggest and best cloud below!"

A gentle breeze whispered, "My dear little cloud,
You may be big, but don't be too proud.
Your size will shrink, as the winds may change,
And your glory will fade, in time's wide range."

But the cloud didn't listen, it floated high,
Trying to reach the sun in the clear, blue sky.
It pushed and it stretched, to be the best,
Until it grew tired, and couldn't rest.

The wind then spoke, "Let go of your pride,
The ego you carry is heavy inside.
When you detach and flow with grace,
You'll find peace and joy in any place."

The little cloud let go, and drifted with ease,
Flowing along, swaying with the breeze.
It found true joy, not in being the best,
But in simply being, free and at rest.

Moral:
Let go of ego and attachment to success or praise. True happiness comes from living freely and without pride.

19. The Gift of Giving

A kind young girl named Sita, so bright,
Saw a poor traveller one cold, dark night.
He had no food, no shelter or warmth,
Sita felt moved to help him, of course.

She ran to her home, with a heart full of care,
And returned with some bread, for the man in despair.
The man took the bread and smiled with delight,
But then said, "You've helped me, now I must take flight."

Sita was puzzled, "Why leave so soon?
Isn't this gift a blessing to you, under the moon?"
The traveller replied, "Your gift was pure,
But what matters most is giving with love, for sure."

"True service is not for praise or fame,
It's a quiet act, without seeking gain.

Give freely, with love, to those in need,
And your heart will bloom, like a beautiful seed."

Sita smiled brightly, for now she could see,
That giving with love was the true key.
No need for rewards, no need for acclaim,
Just serve others with joy, that's the aim.

Moral:
True giving comes from the heart, without expectation of reward. Selfless service brings joy and growth to both giver and receiver.

20. The Dancing Firefly

A little firefly flew through the night,
Blinking and glowing with soft, gentle light.
But she felt so small, in the dark, vast sky,
Thinking, "I am so tiny, I wonder why?"

The stars above twinkled and shined so bright,
And the moon smiled gently, casting her light.
The firefly asked, "How can I be of use,
When the stars and the moon are so full of juice?"

The moon, in her wisdom, spoke down below,
"Dear little one, don't let your light go.
You shine your own way, bright in the dark,
And in doing so, you leave your mark."

"The light you give may seem small to you,
But it makes the darkness a little more blue.
Every tiny glow, every small little spark,
Has a place in the world, lighting up the dark."

So the firefly danced with joy in her heart,
Knowing her glow played a vital part.
She shone with love, in the vast night sky,
For her little light was enough to fly.

Moral:
Never underestimate your own light, no matter how small. Each small act of goodness brightens the world, even in the darkest of times.

21. The Brave Little Sparrow

A little sparrow named Ricky, so small,
Had a dream to fly beyond the great wall.
She looked at the clouds, so high and so wide,
And wondered how to cross to the other side.

But the wall was tall, and the wind was strong,
The sparrow thought, "How can I carry on?"
She asked a wise owl, who perched on a tree,
"How can I fly beyond what I see?"

The owl said gently, "Do not fear the height,
For strength comes from trust, and the will to fight.

The sky is wide, and the path is clear,
But you must trust yourself and push through your fear."

Ricky flapped her wings with courage anew,
She focused on the sky and what she must do.
With faith in her heart and strength in her wings,
She soared through the air, to spread her wings.

The sparrow flew high, beyond the wall,
Her trust and faith made her stand tall.
She reached new heights, beyond her sight,
For faith in yourself is the truest light.

Moral:
With faith and courage, no challenge is too great. Believe in yourself, and you'll find the strength to soar beyond limits.

22. The Silent Mountain

High in the mountains, peaceful and grand,
A mountain stood, silent and unmanned.
It watched the winds, and the rains that came,
And listened quietly, without any claim.

One day, a traveller asked with surprise,
"How can you stand, so still, so wise?
The world moves fast, with noise and haste,
Why do you stay still, with no time to waste?"

The mountain replied in a voice so calm,
"I find peace in silence, in nature's balm.
Though the winds may blow, and the rains may fall,
I stand with stillness, through it all."

"Inner peace comes from being quiet and true,
Not from rushing or seeking what's new.
Listen to your heart, and let silence be,
The greatest strength is found in serenity."

The traveller smiled, and learned that day,
That peace and calm are the truest way.
Like the mountain, he stood still and strong,
Finding silence in a world gone wrong.

Moral:
True strength and peace come from within. Like the mountain, find stillness in the chaos and you'll remain steady and wise without any comparison with others.

23. The Golden Heart

A little girl named Kera, so sweet,
Loved to help others and gave them a treat.
One day she found some golden coins,
Shining and bright, it made her heart join.

She thought, “These coins could buy me so much,
A new dress, some toys, and a golden clutch!”
But then she saw a poor boy nearby,
Hungry and sad, with tears in his eye.

Kera thought for a moment and then said with grace,
“I’ll give him some of these coins, in his time of disgrace.”
She handed it over, with a smile so pure,
Knowing that kindness is the truest cure.

The boy smiled brightly, with thanks in his eyes,
And Anya’s heart soared to the skies.
She learned that the joy in giving, you see,
Is far more precious than anything we can be.

Moral:
True wealth lies in the heart, not in material things. Giving selflessly brings the greatest joy.

24. The Wise Little Deer

A young deer named Bambi, so quick and so light,
Loved to explore in the forest at night.
But she often felt lost, unsure of her way,
Wandering through the woods, day after day.

One evening, she came upon a glowing light,
It was an owl perched high in the night.
"Dear owl," she asked, "I'm always so lost,
How can I find my way without getting tossed?"

The owl replied, "Listen carefully, dear,
Your inner wisdom will always steer.
It's not about rushing or trying to know,
It's about trusting yourself, letting wisdom flow."

"Listen to the silence, hear your heart beat,
Follow your instincts, and stay on your feet.
You'll always find your way, even in the dark,
When you listen to the quiet wisdom that sparks."

Bambi closed her eyes, and her heart knew what to do,
She followed her instincts, steady and true.
And soon, she found her way, without a doubt,
For her inner wisdom had led her out.

Moral:
Listen to the wisdom within. Trust your heart, and it will always guide you in the right direction.

25. The River's Journey

A river named Ganga, flowing so wide,
Tried to control where the water would glide.

She wanted to flow only where she'd choose,
But found that the current would always confuse.

One day, she met a fish who swam with ease,
And asked, "How do you float so calm, like the breeze?"
The fish smiled gently and said, "Oh, dear,
It's not about control, but letting go of fear."

"The river moves freely, in its own pace,
It accepts the flow, and doesn't race.
Life will change, and the current will bend,
But when you let go, your peace won't end."

Ganga listened closely and let go of her strife,
She flowed with the current, embracing life.
And as she moved with grace and ease,
She found joy in simply being the breeze.

Moral:
Life is a flow of changes. The key to peace is letting go and accepting what comes with a calm heart.

26. The Little Mountain

A small mountain named Choti, so proud,
Stood tall in the valley, amidst the clouds.
But one day, a mighty storm came near,
Blowing fierce winds and causing great fear.

The mountain trembled, and thought, "I'm too small,
How can I stand strong against such a fall?"
But then came a gentle voice from the sky,
"It's not the size, but the strength inside that'll fly."

"Storms will come, and winds will roar,
But a mountain stands steady at its core.
It's not about running or trying to flee,
It's standing firm, unshaken, just like me."

Choti took a deep breath and held her ground,
She stood still, though the winds did pound.
And when the storm passed, she still stood tall,
A symbol of strength, despite it all.

Moral:
No matter the size of the obstacle, inner strength and steadfastness will help you overcome anything.

27. The Rainbow's Promise

A rainbow appeared after the rain,
With seven bright colours in its frame.
Each colour was different, bold, and bright,
And each one thought, "I'm the most beautiful sight!"

Red was the brightest, yellow the warmest,
Green was the calmest, blue the purest.
But violet and indigo felt quite small,
Wondering if their colours meant anything at all.

Then the rainbow spoke, with a voice so clear,
"You each have your place, do not fear.
Together you shine, a spectrum so bright,
It's your unity that brings the true light."

"No one colour is more than the rest,
It's the blend of all that makes you the best.
In unity, you'll shine the brightest of all,
A masterpiece painted for one and for all."

The colours now shone in harmony true,
Their beauty came from being one, not few.
And the rainbow brightened the world far and wide,
A symbol of unity, shining with pride.

Moral:
Unity in diversity makes us stronger and more beautiful. Embrace everyone's uniqueness, for together we shine brighter.

28. The Flower's Lesson

A little flower bloomed in the field,
Bright and beautiful, her petals revealed.
She loved the sun, and the rain that came,
And did her best, without seeking fame.

One day, a traveller stopped by her side,
And said, "Oh, flower, you are so bright!
I will pick you, and keep you in my hand,
To show others how lovely you are, so grand."

The flower thought, "Should I bloom for this?
For praise and glory, or a fleeting kiss?"
But then she remembered Ben's word,
And knew her purpose, so she wasn't stirred.

She bloomed for herself, not for the show,
Doing her best, letting love flow.
Whether picked or left, she would not fret,
For her joy came from blooming, and nothing else yet.

The traveller smiled and admired her grace,
But the flower stayed rooted in her place.
She had done her best, and that was enough,
She didn't need praise, for she was already tough.

Moral:
Do your best in everything, not for praise or reward, but because it is your true purpose. Satisfaction lies in the effort, not the result.

29. The Patient Little Sparrow

A little sparrow named Chaya was keen,
To build her nest in a tree so green.
She worked all day, gathering sticks and leaves,
But each time she tried, the wind would deceive.

The twigs would blow away, the leaves would fly,
Chaya would sigh, and look up at the sky.
"I can't build my nest, it's too hard, too tall,
Maybe it's better if I just don't try at all."

But then a voice called, from high in the tree,
It was an old crow, wise as can be.
"Little sparrow, don't give up too soon,
Perseverance brings the sun after the moon."

"Patience is key when the winds are strong,
For after the storm, you'll find your song.
Keep trying, little one, with all your might,
Your nest will be ready, with the morning light."

So Chaya worked patiently, with no rush,
She built her nest, soft as a plush.
The winds may have blown, but she stayed strong,
And in the end, her nest was where she belonged.

Moral:
Patience and perseverance lead to success. Even when things seem hard, keep trying and stay strong.

30. The Little Lamp

A small lamp sat on a shelf so high,
Shining its light, up to the sky.
But it wondered, "What is my purpose, so small?
I shine in the dark, but is that my all?"

One evening, Bryan came by the way,
And noticed the lamp, shining so gay.
He smiled and said, "Little one, don't you know?
Your light comes from within, not from what you show."

"True light shines in the heart, not just outside,
It's the love you give, with no need to hide.
Your light guides others, though it seems small,
In the darkness, it's seen by all."

The lamp glowed brighter, understanding its place,
Shining with love, lighting up the space.
It knew that its purpose was far more than light,
It was to share love, and make things right.

Moral:
True light comes from within. When you shine with love, your inner light will guide others, no matter how small it may seem.

31. The Little Seed's Journey

A tiny seed, so small and shy,
Lay in the soil, beneath the sky.
It thought, "I am small, and no one will see,
How can I grow into something great, like a tree?"

But a wise old tree, with branches so wide,
Spoke softly, as the wind did glide:
"Do not worry, little one, don't feel so small,
Growth happens in silence, and it starts with a call."

"You see, every great tree began as a seed,
It's not the size, but the faith that you need.
Trust in the soil, and the rain that will fall,
And one day, you'll stand tall, so tall."

So the little seed stayed in the ground,
With faith and patience, it knew it was bound.

Days passed, and roots began to spread,
And soon it grew into a tree, full of branches red.

Moral:
Growth takes time, and even the smallest start can lead to something great. Trust the process and be patient as you transform.

32. The Little Butterfly's Lesson

A caterpillar crawled, so slow on the ground,
Dreaming of flying, soaring around.
But one day, it spun a cocoon tight,
And waited inside, through day and night.

The days went by, and the caterpillar thought,
"Will I ever fly? Will I ever be caught?"
But then one day, with a crack and a tear,
A beautiful butterfly emerged from there!

It stretched its wings and flew so high,
Soaring through the clouds and the bright blue sky.
The butterfly smiled and said with grace,
"I was once small, but now I've found my place."

"The change inside me was slow, but true,
And when I trusted, my wings grew too.
Transformation is not easy or fast,
But trust in yourself, and you'll grow at last."

Moral:
True change takes time and patience. Trust in your own transformation, and you will spread your wings when the time is right.

33. The Wise Old Turtle

A young turtle named Mona, so full of cheer,
Rushed through life, with little to fear.
She raced in circles, without a plan,
Trying to keep up with every man.

One day she met a turtle so old,
With a shell so wise, and eyes so bold.
The young turtle asked, "How do you stay so calm,
While the world rushes by like a fast-moving alarm?"

The wise old turtle smiled and said,
"Patience and wisdom guide where you're led.
Life is not about rushing to the end,
It's about taking your time, my dear friend."

"Slow down, listen, and think with your heart,
The answers you seek are not far apart.
Wisdom comes to those who wait,
Who trust the process and don't tempt fate."

Mona slowed down, and began to see,
That wisdom grows from calm and peace, not speed.
She learned to move at her own pace,
And soon found joy in life's slow grace.

Moral:
True wisdom comes from patience and calm. Don't rush through life; take time to enjoy each step.

34. The Courageous Lion Cub

A lion cub, named Simba, so small and shy,
Had dreams of roaring, of soaring high.
But every time he tried, his voice came out weak,
And he wondered, "What makes a lion roar so sleek?"

One day, he met a wise old lion, bold,
Who spoke with a voice, strong and cold:
"Little cub, your roar is inside,
You must believe in it, not hide."

"Your strength is not in the sound of your roar,
But in the heart that beats deep at your core.
Believe in yourself, and the world will see,
The mighty lion you are meant to be."

Simba took a deep breath and roared with might,
And the jungle trembled, bathed in light.

He learned that courage comes from within,
And believing in yourself is where you begin.

Moral:
Believe in your own strength and potential. Courage comes from within, and once you trust yourself, you can achieve great things.

35. The Grateful Tree

A tree stood tall, with branches wide,
Its leaves shimmered in the sun, open wide.
One day, a bird came to rest in the tree,
And asked, "Dear tree, what makes you so free?"

The tree replied with a voice so deep,
"I stand here grateful, and I don't weep.
For every branch, every leaf, every root,
I'm thankful for the sun and the rain that shoots."

The bird looked puzzled and said with a smile,
"Tell me more, dear tree, I'll stay for a while."
The tree whispered softly, "Gratitude's key,
It's the foundation of joy, you see."

"Gratitude turns simple things into gold,
It's the magic that makes the heart bold.
Be thankful for all that you have each day,
And you'll find happiness along the way."

The bird flew away, filled with delight,
And thanked the tree as it took flight.
The tree stood still, with a heart so full,
Grateful for all, both big and small.

Moral:
Gratitude is the key to a joyful heart. Be thankful for what you have, and happiness will follow.

36. The Honest Gardener

A gardener named Jimmy worked with care,
Planting seeds, nurturing them with prayer.
One day, he found a small, hidden sprout,
But he noticed it wasn't what he'd set out.

The plant was different, not like the others,
But Jimmy thought, “I’ll tell no one, not even my brothers.”
He hid the plant, hoping no one would see,
Afraid of what they’d think about his garden's plea.

But then Binny appeared, with a smile so wide,
And asked, “Jimmy, why do you try to hide?”
The gardener confessed, "I’ve made a mistake,
I planted a wrong seed, for goodness’ sake!"

Binny said gently, “It’s okay, my friend,
Truthfulness is where the healing begins.
Don’t fear mistakes, or the things you’ve done wrong,
For honesty is where the heart grows strong.”

Jimmy smiled, and spoke with grace,
Telling the truth about the plant in place.
And to his surprise, it thrived and grew,
For honesty brought a blessing too.

Moral:
Truthfulness is powerful. Don’t hide your mistakes; honesty leads to growth and healing.

37. The Moon and the Stars

The moon shone brightly, high in the sky,
With stars twinkling softly as they passed by.
But the moon felt lonely, and thought with a sigh,
“I am big and bright, yet the stars are so spry.”

“I wish I could twinkle, I wish I could dance,
Like the stars up above, in their sparkling trance.”
But the stars, they laughed, “Dear moon, so wise,
You already shine, right before our eyes.”

“You’re the queen of the night, the ruler of the sky,
Without you, the night would pass by.
We twinkle and shine, but only because of you,
Your steady light makes the world anew.”

The moon smiled brightly, and found her peace,
For in her heart, all her longing ceased.
She realized then, contentment comes,
When you embrace who you are, and all that’s to come.

Moral:
Be content with who you are. Each person has their own unique light, and comparing yourself to others only dims that light.

38. The Humble Bamboo

A bamboo stalk stood tall and proud,
Among the trees that reached for the clouds.
"I am the strongest," said the bamboo,
"No tree is as mighty, no tree as true."

A mighty storm came, strong and fierce,
With winds that howled and rain that pierced.
The bamboo stood firm, trying not to bend,
But the winds were too strong to defend.

The oak tree stood firm, without a bend,
While the bamboo, with a soft sway, met the wind.
It bent with the storm, not fighting the force,
And stood back up when the storm ran its course.

The oak tree groaned, "Why did you bend so low?
You could have stood strong, like me, you know."

The bamboo smiled gently and said,
"It's my humility that keeps me ahead."

"I bend, but I do not break,
I flex with the storm, for my own sake.
In humility, I find my might,
For the strongest tree knows when to bend, not fight."

Moral:
True strength lies in flexibility and humility

39. The Value Of Humility

A king named Raj ruled the land,
With a mighty army at his command.
He wore a crown, with jewels so bright,
And thought of himself as the greatest knight.

One day, an old sage came to the palace door,
And asked the king, "What do you truly adore?"
The king said, "I have everything, I am so grand,
I rule the land, and hold the future in my hand."

The sage smiled kindly and said,
"True greatness comes when ego is shed.
You may rule the land, but your heart must be pure,
For humility and kindness are the things that endure."

King Raj was puzzled, but listened with care,
And realized then, life's not always fair.

He gave up his crown, and walked humbly through,
Understanding now, that ego must be few.

He helped the people, both near and far,
And shone brighter than any royal star.
For the greatest king is humble and wise,
And rules with love, not ego or lies.

Moral:
True greatness comes from humility and love, not pride or power. Lead with kindness and wisdom.

40. The Kind Deer

A deer named Bambi roamed the field,
With gentle steps, and a heart unsealed.
She loved all creatures, both big and small,
And treated them kindly, one and all.

One day, she saw a fox in distress,
Caught in a net, unable to progress.
Bambi approached and said with care,
"I will help you, for I cannot bear,
To see anyone suffer, or in pain,
For compassion is the heart's true gain."

She nibbled the net and freed the fox,
Who smiled and said, "You're the greatest ox!"
But Bambi laughed, and said with grace,
"Kindness is the gift we all must embrace."

The fox thanked her and ran on ahead,
And Bambi's heart was filled with stead.
For she knew that love and care will find,
A place in the heart, and peace of mind.

Moral:
Compassion and kindness are the greatest gifts. Help others, and you will find joy in your own heart.

41. The Diligent Squirrel

A little squirrel named Bittu was small,
But she worked so hard, giving it her all.
She gathered acorns, storing them away,
For the coming winter, the cold and gray.

One day, a rabbit asked, "Why do you work,
When the weather is warm and the leaves still perk?"
Bittu smiled and said, "I work now, dear friend,
For tomorrow's need is what I must tend."

"The future is uncertain, but we can prepare,
By doing our best and showing we care.
Hard work today makes the future bright,
And in the end, it feels just right."

The rabbit, now thoughtful, hopped away,
And worked a little harder, day by day.
For he understood what Bittu had said,
That diligence today will prepare the path ahead.

Moral:
Hard work and responsibility today will prepare you for tomorrow. Plan ahead, and you'll be ready for whatever comes.

42. The Wise Old Owl

A wise old owl sat high in a tree,
Watching the world with a calm, steady plea.
One day, a young bird flew by so fast,
And asked the owl, "Why do you sit so still, at last?"

The owl smiled gently, and said with ease,
“I don’t rush around, nor do I tease.
I observe, I reflect, and I learn each day,
For wisdom comes to those who wait and stay.”

“Knowledge is not just from books or words,
It comes from silence and the world you observe.
When you listen deeply, and think with care,
The answers you seek are always there.”

The young bird learned, and took to heart,
That wisdom grows when you take time to start.
The owl flew silently into the night,
And the young bird learned to seek out the light.

Moral:
Knowledge and wisdom come from stillness, observation, and reflection. Take time to listen and learn.

43. The Lonely Mountain

A mountain stood tall, all covered in snow,
It watched the valley far below.
It said, "I am lonely, with no one around,
I am just here, without a sound."

One day, the wind came blowing through,
Whistling past, so strong and true.
It said, "Mountain, why do you sigh?
You are strong and grand, don’t wonder why."

The mountain replied, "I’m so still and alone,
While others are busy, I’m here on my own."
The wind laughed softly and said, "You see,
Your strength is in your stillness, naturally."

"You stand so tall, so calm, and grand,
Your strength comes from the earth and sand.
Do not long for what others may have,
For your power lies in your own path."

The mountain stood still, and found its peace,
Knowing its strength would never cease.

It stood proudly, silent and tall,
For it knew now that being still was its call.

Moral:
True strength comes from within, and sometimes it's found in stillness, not in constant movement or comparison.

44. Embrace change with Grace

A stream flowed gently, winding and clear,
But sometimes it would stop, filled with fear.
"I don't want to change," the stream would say,
"I want to stay the same, day by day."

One day, a wise old tree by the shore,
Spoke softly, "Little stream, don't fear change anymore.
Change is part of life, as sure as the sun,
Embrace it, for it's what makes you run."

"Change helps you grow, helps you expand,
It's the force that shapes the rocks in the land.
By moving forward, you'll find new paths,
And discover strength that will surely last."

The stream paused, and then it flowed,
It let go of fear and down the path it strode.
It embraced the changes that came its way,
And knew it was stronger every day.

Moral:
Change is inevitable and can bring growth and strength. Embrace it with grace and openness.

45. The Lazy Donkey

A donkey named Golu loved to sleep,
Lying in the meadow, just counting sheep.

"I don't need to work, or carry a load,
I'll sit here in the sun, along the road."

One day, a farmer came, needing help,
To carry hay to his barn, with a yelp.
"Golu, dear donkey, can you help me today?
There's work to be done, don't sleep, I say!"

But Golu yawned and said, "I'm too tired, you see,
I'll rest, and you can do it for me."
The farmer sighed and walked away,
His work undone, for the donkey's dismay.

The next day, Golu saw the others at work,
The cows, the horses, they never would shirk.
They worked hard, with no time to rest,
And Golu realized that effort is best.

He worked with the farmer, helping each day,
And found that hard work led to success, in every way.
He learned that laziness does not last,
And hard work brings results, both slow and fast.

Moral:
Hard work leads to success. Don't wait for things to come to you—put in the effort and you'll see results.

46. The Little Leaf

A little leaf named Ritu grew on a tree,
She loved the warm sun, and the breeze so free.
She watched the seasons change, one by one,
And wondered why she had to be so still under the sun.

One day, the wind came with a soft whisper,
"Ritu, little leaf, it's time to remember:
Life is full of cycles, both big and small,
And letting go is the key to it all."

Ritu asked, "But I love where I am,
Why must I fall when it's part of the plan?"

The wind replied, “When you let go and fall,
You make room for new leaves, one and all.”

And so, Ritu let go and drifted away,
Knowing her letting go would be okay.
She became part of the earth, so deep,
And in her fall, new life began to leap.

Moral:
Letting go is part of life’s cycle. Sometimes, to grow, we must release what no longer serves us.

47. The Brave Little Fish

A little fish named Vision lived in the sea,
Afraid to swim deep, where the currents were free.
"Why is the ocean so dark and wide?
I’m scared to swim, there’s nowhere to hide."

One day, a wise turtle came near,
And said to Vision, “Have no fear.
The ocean is vast, but it’s full of light,
You must dive deep to see what’s right."

"The deepest waters hold treasures untold,
But you’ll never find them if you stay on the shore.
Don’t let fear keep you from what you could see,
The beauty of the ocean, the world, and you—so free!"

Vision listened, and with courage so bright,
She swam deeper into the endless night.
She found coral reefs, and seashells galore,
And knew that the ocean had so much more.

Moral:
Overcome fear and doubt, for facing challenges opens the door to new experiences and discoveries.

48. The Wise Spider

A spider named Squiky spun a beautiful web,
She worked with skill, no task was too ebb.
One day, a fly flew into the net,
Caught by the threads, unable to forget.

The fly cried, “How did you make this so strong?
It’s perfect and beautiful, I did no wrong!”
Squiky smiled and said, “It’s my art, you see,
I spun it with care, every thread is key."

“Creativity comes with time and effort,
And the work is worth it, that’s what I assert.
When you work with focus, your dreams will unfold,
Like this web, which is both strong and bold.”

The fly admired the web, then flew away,
Knowing that hard work makes dreams come to stay.
And Squiky kept spinning her webs with pride,
For creativity and effort are keys to the tide.

Moral:
Creativity and hard work lead to beautiful results. Dedication to your craft brings success.

49. The Silly Goose

A silly goose named Nitu was quick to speak,
He never thought twice, always so meek.
One day, he saw a wise old owl,
Sitting on a branch, so calm and foul

"Why do you sit there, not flying about?
I am free, soaring in and out!"
The owl replied, "I've learned with time,
That wisdom is better than an empty rhyme."

"Just flying around and making a fuss,
Will never bring peace or wisdom, thus.
You must think before you act or speak,
Only then will your future be truly sleek."

Nitu thought hard, then flapped his wings,
And tried to be wise in the small things.
Now, he listens and thinks before he speaks,
And has grown wiser, week after week.

Moral:
Think before you leap. Think carefully before acting or speaking.

50. The Loyal Dog

A dog named Jimmy followed his master,
Faithfully through life, no matter the faster.
He walked beside him through thick and thin,
Always loyal, with a joyful grin.

One day, his master stumbled and fell,
Jimmy barked loudly, and rang a bell.
He ran to his side, not a moment too soon,
And helped him rise, under the moon.

The master smiled, and said with pride,
"Your loyalty has been my guide.
You are a friend, true and kind,
In you, true loyalty I always find."

And so Jimmy's love and faith stayed true,
For loyalty brings joy, and friendships too.

Moral:
Loyalty and faithfulness create strong, lasting bonds. Always be there for those you love.

51. The Giving Tree

A young tree named Fruity grew in the grove,
She loved the forest, the sun, and the cove.
One day, a traveller came passing by,
And asked the tree, "Can you help me? I'm dry."

Fruity stretched out her branches so wide,
And offered shade on the traveller's side.
Years went by, and the traveller returned,
Fruity gave him fruit, for which he yearned.

"I don't have much, but I will share,
Everything I have, I give with care."
The tree gave her leaves, her fruit, and her wood,
To help the traveller, as she knew she should.

As time passed, Fruity grew old and worn,
But the traveller returned, tired and torn.
"I don't need shade or food, my dear tree,"
He said, "I just need to rest, can you see?"

Fruity gave her last branch, so pure,
And the traveller smiled, knowing for sure,
That the greatest joy comes from giving,
For the more you give, the more you're living.

Moral:
The joy of giving is endless. Generosity creates lasting happiness.

52. The Helping Squirrel

A squirrel named Squiky lived in a grand tree,
She loved to play, running so free.
One winter, the forest turned cold,
And many animals had nothing to hold.

A rabbit came by, trembling with fear,
“I have no food, and the cold is near."
Squiky, with kindness, gave her some seeds,
To help her survive, fulfil her needs.

"I have plenty," said Squiky with a smile,
"Take what you need, and rest for a while."
The rabbit thanked her, and stayed in her home,
Warm and safe from the cold's dome.

Spring came again, and the snow did melt,
But Squiky didn’t expect anything to be dealt.
She just smiled, knowing in her heart,
That helping others is the true art.

Moral:
Helping others without expecting anything in return creates true joy and happiness.

53. The Wise Farmer

A farmer named Mannu worked the land,
With simple tools and an open hand.
He grew his crops, tended his field,
And found contentment in all that it yielded.

One day, a merchant came to his door,
"Why do you live so simply, and ask for no more?
I can offer you riches, treasures untold,
If you work with me, your wealth will unfold."

But Mannu smiled and shook his head,
"I am rich already, in what I've been fed.
Contentment is the treasure I seek,
For happiness comes not from being sleek."

The merchant left, still searching for more,
While Mannu worked on, content at the core.
He had all he needed, and nothing was missed,
For simplicity brings the greatest bliss.

Moral:
True wealth is found in contentment, not in material possessions. Live simply, and happiness will follow.

54. The Proud Peacock

A peacock named Pipi was proud of his tail,
He strutted and danced, in colours so pale.
One day, he saw a humble dove,
With simple feathers, but a heart full of love.

"Why do you stay so plain, my dear?"
Asked Pipi, "Your beauty isn't clear.
Look at my feathers, how they shine so bright,
I'm the most beautiful creature in sight!"

The dove smiled gently and said with grace,
"True beauty lies in the heart, not in the face.
Pride can fade, but kindness remains,
And love brings beauty in all its veins."

Pipi paused and thought, then bowed his head,
He understood the dove, and no longer fled.
He learned that beauty comes from within,
And humility brings true joy to begin.

Moral:
Humility is greater than pride. True beauty comes from within, and kindness shines brighter than appearance.

55. The Wise Warrior's Victory

In a village far away, on a mountain tall,
Lived a brave young warrior, the strongest of them all.
His name was Wisi, with muscles so grand,
He was known as the mightiest in the land.

He trained every day, with sword and with shield,
His strength was unmatched, on every battlefield.
But there came a challenge, one stormy night,
That would test his power, his wisdom, and might.

The village was called to the great hall to hear,
Of a fearsome beast that would soon draw near.
A dragon, they said, with scales shining bright,
And fiery breath that could scorch the night.

The villagers trembled, unsure what to do,
But Wisi stood up, brave and true.
"I'll face this dragon," he said with a grin,
"My strength will defeat it, I'll surely win!"

He set off to find the dragon so fierce,
With sword in his hand and heart full of cheer.

But when he arrived, to his great surprise,
The dragon sat waiting with sad, lonely eyes.

"I am not here to fight," the dragon said,
"Nor to burn and destroy, nor to leave you dead.
I am cursed by a spell, by a wizard so mean,
To live in this cave, unseen and unclean."

Wisi lowered his sword, confusion in his heart,
He thought for a moment, then had a fresh start.
"I don't need my strength," he said with a smile,
"To help you, dear dragon, let me think for a while."

Wisi sat down beside the dragon's cave,
And asked, "Tell me your story, I want to be brave."
The dragon began with a voice soft and deep,
And Wisi listened closely, no secret to keep.

The tale was of loneliness, of magic and pain,
A spell gone wrong, that caused endless strain.
"I've never had a friend, I've only had fear,
And now I am stuck, year after year."

Wisi thought and thought, and then had a plan,
He didn't need strength—he needed to understand.
"I'll help break your curse, I'll find the right way,
But first, let's be friends, starting today."

So Wisi spoke to the wizard, with kindness and grace,
And with clever words, he found the right place.
He broke the spell, and the dragon was free,
And together they laughed, as happy as could be.

When Wisi returned, the villagers cheered,
But Wisi knew the truth, what he'd truly feared.
"It is not the strength of the body that wins,
But the strength of the mind, where true victory begins."

The dragon, now a friend, flew high in the sky,
And Wisi learned that sometimes, the wisest reply,
Is not to fight, but to listen and learn,
For kindness and wisdom are what we must earn.

So remember this story, **"YOUNG WARRIORS"** bright,
True strength comes from the heart, not just might.
For a warrior's victory, on land or on sea,
Is won with the mind, and the heart full of glee.

Moral :
It is not the strength of the body but the strength of the mind that determines a warrior's victory.

56. Silence Speaks the Loudest

David and Alice, friends so true,
But their reactions were quite askew.
Leo, the best with arrogance bright,
Teased them both, with all his might.

David stayed calm, he didn't engage,
Kept his cool, no matter the stage.
Leo's words, sharp as a knife,
Couldn't shake David, who led a quiet life.

Alice, though, with pride in her chest,
Boasted and challenged, saying, "I'm the best!"
"I'll beat Leo," she boldly declared,
But her focus was lost, and she wasn't prepared.

When the results were finally out,
David excelled, leaving no doubt.
Leo, astonished, could hardly believe,
His arrogance didn't help him achieve.

Alice, who boasted, found to her dismay,
Her grades had worsened, despite what she'd say.
David's silence spoke louder than words,
His actions, like music, were sweet as the birds.

Moral :
So remember this lesson, both humble and wise:
Let your actions speak louder than your lies.
In the end, it's effort, not boastful cheer,
That will bring you success year after year.

57. Money : Blessing or curse

Ben and Shane were brothers.

Ben was very ambitious, he decided to go to the city;

And earn a living.

His aim was to become very rich, from the very beginning.

But Shane was very loving and courteous;

Towards his old parents and everyone near and dear.

Shane decided to stay in the village.

He wanted to serve his old parents and earn a living.

To fulfil the bare necessities of life, both;

This was Shane's will.

With time, Shane started earning handsomely.

Of course, also serving his parents happily.

But the story was not so beautiful for Ben.

Ben lost his job for all the wrong reasons.

Ben also the little money he had;

Prior to going to the city.

Famished, Ben returned home.

Shane welcomed Ben.

Shane invited Ben to join his work.

And the whole family, lived happily ever after.

Together Ben and Shane worked and left a mark,

A mark of success in both serving their parents,

And carrying out daily work.

Moral:
Money can buy a lot of things, but not everything. Money cannot buy love, especially that of parents.

58. Compassion

There was a boy called Leo.

He was from a royal family.

But still he had a bad habit unfortunately;

He had the habit of stealing.

Not far away there was a boy called Rio.

He was from a poor family.

But still he had the habit of giving heartily.

One day Leo and Rio went for a picnic together.

Leo stole Rio's piece of cake.

Leo lied to Rio that he had forgotten to bring his food.

Rio smiled compassionately,

And searched for his food to share it with Leo.

Seeing this Leo was embarrassed.

Quickly he confessed to Rio, what he had done.

Rio grabbed his friend and said "Forget it; Dear friend".

Both shared their food.

Isn't the ending of the story very good.

Moral :
Be compassionate and share whatever little you have and live together happily.

59. Master of One Art.

Rick and Hick were two young buddies.

Both were good in studies.

Rick also liked painting, dancing, singing.

So accordingly, Rick spent time in practising;

All that was to his liking.

Hick however, was only good in studies.

With time, Hick improved in academics.

Ultimately he became a professor in a big university.

But on the other hand, Rick could not excel in any field.

He got a tag of mediocrity.

Moral :
Be expert in only one job;
The mediocre level is overcrowded,
Aim for the top.

60. Arrogance: A pitfall

Ela and Eva were two sisters.

They loved each other very much.

Time passed by, Ela and Eva grew into two beautiful girls.

Both started searching for a job for a living.

Ela quickly got a job, but Eva did not.

After Ela got the job, she started neglecting Eva.

Ultimately Ela separated from Eva.

One fine morning, Ela was fired from her job for treason.

Ela started searching for a job to make her ends meet, for a reason.

One day Ela, went for an interview.

As she entered the interview room, Ela was astonished.

The person who was holding the interview was;

None other than Eva, her sister;

Whom Ela had from her mind, long ago banished,.

Ela felt humiliated, she knew she could not get the job.

But after the interview, Eva congratulated Ela.

Because Ela had qualified the interview on merit; Alas!

Ela was dumbstruck.

Arrogance had changed Ela before,

But now, she could not believe her luck.

Moral :
Arrogance leads to one's downfall.

61. Avoid bad Friends.

Steve was a good boy.

But sometimes he carried out small mischiefs;

At home, with his toys.

So his parents decided to send him to a boarding school.

Steve started his life in hostel as a rule.

It was here where he met Vicky, a naughty boy.

Steve and Vicky became good friends.

But alas! In the company of Vicky, the naughty boy;

Steve became a victim of notorious ploy.

Steve started taking intoxication.

Steve's parents soon came to know of this habit.

Steve's parents decided to bring him back home.

Once at home, Steve stopped taking intoxication.

Steve's parents breathed a sigh of relief.

Their child was now in front of their eyes.

Steve was once again their small, simple boy.

They had this strong belief.

Moral :
Long association with bad friends leaves an impelling impact on our minds and destroys our character.

62. Higher Perspective towards Life

Bryan and Aryan were brothers.

Bryan and Aryan enjoyed, playing cricket together.

But Aryan was sometimes omitted;

By Bryan's friends while playing cricket,.

Bryan and Aryan soon grew up.

Later Bryan got selected for the National Cricket Cup.

But Aryan could not make it, since from his childhood.

He had been neglected.

But Aryan did not get discouraged.

He looked at it from a higher perspective.

He sincerely completed his formal education;

Shattering all his critics.

But Bryan left his formal education mid-way.

Bryan started playing for the national team.

But one day, misfortune struck Bryan.

He lost an eye while playing cricket.

Aryan, on the other hand,

Got a good job in a multinational company;

With a fat packet

Moral :
We should view things from a higher perspective, just as an eagle watches from above the clouds, whereas the other birds flying below, search for shelter during the rain.

63. Lamenting does not pay

Michael and Andy were the captains of two soccer teams.

In a tournament, both Michael's team;

And Andy's team participated.

In the initial stages Michael's men won all the matches;

Undefeated!

Michael was on the top of the world.

Andy's team won only a few matches.

But Andy did not get discouraged.

He put in more effort every next match.

However, both qualified;

For the final match of the tournament.

On the final day, Andy's team won the match;

Applying every technique in their armament.

Moral :
We should not lament after loss, we should rather prepare ourselves to hit the next target.

64. Lies : Good or bad

Archie and Richie were both good friends.

Archie was from a royal family, Richie was from a poor one.

They were once wandering in the woods.

All of a sudden, right in front of them;

Some thugs stood.

Archie was dressed in royal clothes and jewels.

The thugs looted Archie.

But all of a sudden;

The thugs' eyes lit up with more greed.

The thugs asked Richie, "Whether Archie;

Was from a royal family breed?"

Richie quickly figured out that;

If he tells the truth, the thugs would abduct his friend, Archie.

Richie lied that for a dance drama, they were preparing.

Hence Archie had dressed himself like "Prince Charming".

Luckily the thugs left.

Never mind the theft.

Moral :
We should never lie, but if a lie saves an innocent person from distress then, lying is not an offence.

65. Obstacles: Boon or bane

Gary was the father of a young, handsome boy named Lary.

Gary once brought two small plants.

Gary asked Lary to plant one of them outside the house;

And the other inside.

Days passed by, Lary became busy in his daily chores.

Suddenly one day, Gary asked his son, Lary;

To observe both plants.

Lary observed that the plant inside the house;

Was frail with dry leaves.

Whereas the plant outside;

Had a luxuriant growth.

Gary explained to Lary;

The hot sun, the rain, the gushing wind;

Had made the plant outside strong.

Whereas the plant inside the house;

Although did not had to face, the burning sun, rain, wind,

Had grown into a frail plant.

Similarly obstacles might come in life,.

But they need to be tackled;

Because tackling problems make us strong;

Both mentally and physically.

Moral :
Obstacles in life may make a person distressed temporarily, but in the long run makes the person versatile in all aspects.

66. Enemy or Friend, who is better?

Tim and Dim were classmates.

Tim was great in academics, Dim was weak.

Tim and Dim were at daggers drawn, both freaks.

Tim used to taunt Dim, compared him with a donkey.

Dim had a friend named Paul; quite funky.

Paul used to console Dim whenever Tim taunted him.

Paul used to give company to Dim while playing videos games;

Movies & films.

Paul however, never encouraged Dim to focus on studies.

But, Dim could not take it anymore from Tim.

So, he decided to improve his academics.

When the final results were declared for the academic year;

Dim had passed with flying colours, especially in mathematics.

Dim thanked Tim for his misbehaviour.

Tim was dumbstruck;

How could Dim change his gear!

Moral :
A clever enemy is better than a foolish friend.

67. Urgent Work First

Sita and Gita were two good friends.

Once, unknowingly both of them got infected and fell ill.

Unfortunately their exams were approaching;

Which was a big deal.

Sita's parents advised her to take medicine and rest.

Sita, who was more intelligent than Gita;

Accepted her parents' advice, like a good girl.

But Gita, who was a fool;

Did not follow the advice of her parents and lost her cool.

Gita neglected her health and did not take any medicine.

Gita focussed on her lessons, soon she became too lean.

On the day of the exam, Sita went to school;

And gave her exam with energy; full.

Gita on the other hand, felt feeble and ill;

She could not give her exam,

And her life came to stand-still.

Moral :
Urgent and important work should be attended / done first.

68. Price of Disrespect

Silver and Gulliver were two friends from a royal family.

Silver was arrogant, proud, envious, actually.

Gulliver was humble, non-envious, personally.

Silver once visited a departmental store;

After collecting the goods;

He threw the money on the table of the store owner;

Who was sitting near the exit door.

Gulliver visited the same store, the next day.

After collecting all necessities, he kept the cash humbly;

On the table of the store owner in a gentle way.

And wished him "Merry Christmas!"

The store owner was so moved by Gulliver's humility;

That he refused to take the price of the goods from Gulliver.

Even though Gulliver insisted; really

Moral :
We should respect everybody accordingly to their position in society. Disrespect out of pride and envy leads to our downfall.

69. Greed makes us bleed

Denis was a young, handsome lad.

One fine morning, he found a precious gem;

Lying on the lane, what luck he had!

A thug saw the entire incident.

He introduced himself to Denis.

He bluffed to Denis, that he possessed;

A costlier gem than Denis, what a ploy!

The thug gave a fake gem to Denis.

Denis took it, but on second thought;

Denis assumed the thug certainly;

Possessed a costlier gem, in stock.

The thug convinced Denis that;

He would give a better gem to Denis, provided;

Denis gave him the gem he found on the lane.

Denis agreed, as his eyes lit up with greed.

The precious gem was taken by the thug;

Denis was hence tricked, a situation;

He could not duck.

Moral:
There is enough in this world for a man's need, but not enough for his greed.

70. Anger leads to doom

Charlie and Harlie were two brothers.

Charlie was short-tempered whereas;

Harlie was cool and calm.

Once their aunt Paula, gifted each of them a wrist-watch;

And also brought for them, chocolate fudge.

Charlie and Harlie had a caretaker named John.

Once John, found their wrist-watches unattended, at dawn.

He could not control the urge;

To steal each of the jewelled watch.

When Charlie came to know that his watch was stolen;

Insane with anger he threatened;

www.ingramcontent.com/pod-product-compliance
Lightning Source LLC
LaVergne TN
LVHW071146160826
845679LV00003B/575